IN OUR TERRIBLENESS

(Some elements and meaning in black style)

IMAMU AMIRI BARAKA

(LeRoi Jones)

and

FUNDI

(Billy Abernathy)

THE BOBBS-MERRILL COMPANY, INC.

Indianapolis   New York

ACKNOWLEDGMENTS

Acknowledgment is made to the following publishers for permission to reprint the specified poems:

"All in the Street" first appeared in *Black Dialogue* and is reprinted by permission.

"Answers in Progress" first appeared in *Tales*, published by Grove Press, and is reprinted by permission.

"Jihad" first appeared in the *Poster Poem Series* and is reprinted by permission.

"Dazed and out of their Wool Heads" first appeared in *Umoja* and is reprinted by permission.

The Bobbs-Merrill Company, Inc.
A Subsidiary of Howard W. Sams & Co., Inc.
Publishers / Indianapolis · Kansas City · New York

FOR ALL THE ADVOCATES OF KAWAIDA

FOR THE ADVOCATES—

TEACH KAWAIDA!!

IN OUR TERRIBLENESS

Some terrible

folks

these inside here.

As the flower turns

the climb thru space to God

that

consciousness

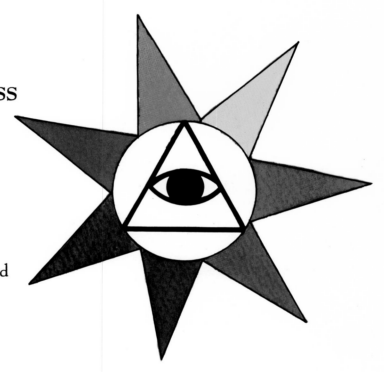

Revelation

As a

fact
    The Pictures
    The Images
    The Lovers THEMSELVES

    LOOK AT THEM

        force
        at YOU

The living force

Terribleness
Bloods!
Brothers

Hipsters

Old Folks

Kids

Roots

A LONG IMAGE STORY IN MOTION

PAPERMOTION
    PITCHAS ABOUT THE SON
        OF BLACK MAN. . . . .

Who inhabits the cities possesses the thrust of life to power.
The family unit. The man will get his woman. They are de signs.
And the kidz is the whole cycle. An old man looks one way
(dig it, the language) An old man *looks one way*—his yng son
looks another.

    Man woman child in a house is a nation. More than them
we become large cities that shd have, domes, spires, spirals,
pyramids, you need somthin flashy man. Some red and bright
green or yr black self. The cities the cities our dominion.
We first built them and we will manage to build them some'gin

Terribleness – Our beauty is BAD cause we bad. Bad things.
Some bad bad bad ass niggers.

Ask Me What I Am—
The rhythm of beings is the reason for being.
The sanity of form is allness wholeness rightness
nigger love a magic being
the dipping interior resurrect constant continuous
the way the nigger walk

The red hat is a magic hat
the razor a sword flasher
the lines of adepts all niggers really
the pyramid speaks of niggers actually
the word will be given by niggers
we are in our most holy selves niggers
god is a nigger really
ask who god is and he will answer if you ask right

nigger is a definition of the wholly detached from material
consideration a nigger dont have no gold
not even a negro got gold but a negro think like he would if he
had gold
a nigger is holy

a nigger is killer and builder struts frantic for love
nigger is a frantic love man hippity hoppity 7 sided figure
the nigger who i am
who is my self and father mother your self
deep man
my man

my main man

my main main man

we niggers together
forever

raise.

Since there is a "good" we know is bullshit, corny as Lawrence Welk On Venus, we will not be that hominy shit. We will be, definitely, bad, bad, as a mother-fucker.

"That's a bad vine that dude got on."

"Damn."

"Its a bad dude."

IMAGE

To carry a self through all (motives) motifs the weird world
offers as other than old or corny reality tho is stone, reality
is reality, *everythings for real*.

Our terribleness is our survival as beautiful beings, any where.
Who can dig that? Any where, even flying through space like we
all doing, even faced with the iceman, the abominable snowman,
the beast for whom there is no answer, but change in fire light
and heat for the world

To be bad is one level
But to be terrible, is to be
badder dan nat

Terribleness
Terribleness
Terribleness
Terribleness   (capable of terror
                                                 producement
                                          production prod
                                      to terror terroristicism
                            "The Blood" Ahhhh he so hip.

The Images are *stops* of the organ life.

Carry the religion through years to our sight. Our

place. Where we plays It is all a play, of

illusion and memory God remembering that he is

always him Not idle looks these halls yawn

as we circle always toward light A shape of

energy our memory of him us

                Bloods
                The Blood
                The fellahs   (een there
                                                 fellaheen
                                                 Bedouin
                                                 Black Arab
                                                 Hamitic Arab
                                                 Moor
                                                 Muslim
                                                 African

The chemists lounge plotting their return to

power. From "the furtherest extreme of material existence."

Re Turn. Regarding your change, my man. It is there

to be taken.

Image in the street Strength in the Image Love in the

bust light like time mass concealed plastic memory hurts as

an ecstasy return re change re God re look perfection

The perfection of our confidence in body body flies

spins the sun laughs at it Sonafabitch he

points a drum with night his arm hanging off

him a black long coat scary.

African African African
African Black Jesus
       Black Ham (Kam Cam Chem-Changer Chemist
       Black Moses
       Black Egypt
       Black Pythagoras
       Black Aesop

With a pulled down humpy hat a feather a slow jungle bunny

bend to him black egypt black sphinx black pharoah

Sun calls to his kingdom to come again black magic black sense

There are mostly portraits here. Portraits of life. Of life
being lived. Black People inspire us. Send life into us. Draw
it in. Lead more energy in. From themselves Thru to the Being
From the Being to The Being. In Our Terribleness. We wanted to
conjure with Black Life to recreate it for our selves. So that the
connection with you would be a bigger Self. Abernathy has many
many photos each "bad" in some aspect. Abernathy is himself, a
terrible terbul dude. The way the terribleness of us gets thru
thru him to us, again. The artist completing the cycle recreating.

ORDER OF SERVICE

In the Sun School the mystics of Egypt, our fathers,

studied to make the pyramidal inch

reflect the destiny of humans on earth.

The date 2188, approximate fall of the

Western empires, to complete ruin. If

they had not "magnetized

to love." Mourn

Pray,

New "Macedonia",

will surely

come.

Mourn that we are here

Pray that the Morn will not be

worse.

Pray that we are not part of the Western

Empire, in soul.

We know we are not.

In Our Terribleness

We know exactly

Who We Are.

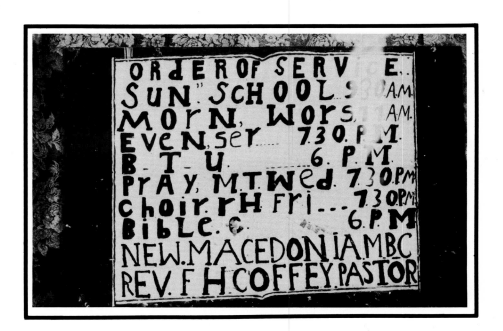

They had us in a cage.

To hold back our rage. Our eyes

smiled

Anyway

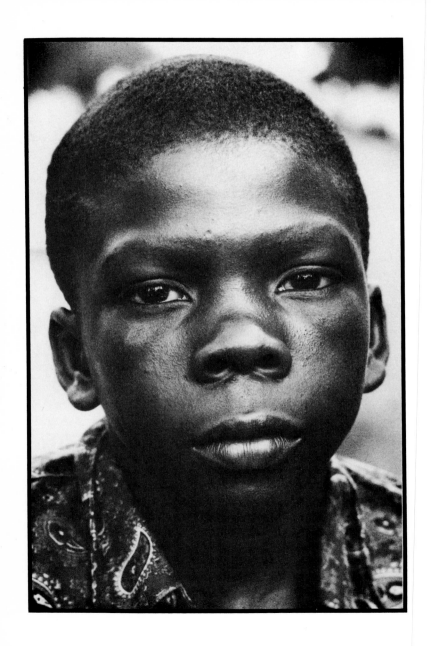

You shd been there man

like you shda been eatin sun

   (just

   dont get in the way,

man

All these are in the hipness shown. The triumph of our way.

All these are together. Dont ever fuck with me. An emblem

of breath. Can you dig a fist, so beautiful??

SISTERS

Was this the highest of the physical

I was answering the truth of the whole

She was beautiful in your mind, Halisi, Burnt

full of light. So it is a spiritual blessing

to see eyes and nose and mouth so,

perfect.

We try to move from the known of our selves the deepest known

which is our black cord of dazzle. We are thoroughly ashamed to

be slaves. But that is simple. And the starting block of anything.

We whizzed from there. The baton we pass to the bloods. The simbas.

The magical Soul of the Blood. All this will be taught in a school

before the century ends. They will begin to institutionalize our

climb, our rule, and the love of peace to come.

Hey, man, look at this woman.

She is fine. Fine.

I cant say nothing else.

We need to give her something.

I love you black perfect woman. Your spirit will rule the twenty first century.

This is why we ourselves speed to grace.

Get back our truth. Babeee you was fine with grease in yo head

but with yo own thing goin youse past any thing

Big Eyes got to be filled with love. Abernathy say

"More Than All"

The pure image of the black woman. The Nation of Islam. To Raise the Race. This is a value system the Honorable Elijah Muhammad has created out of Negritude and Islam to defend and develop black people.

So our sisters floating in to us faces in the soft blankness of spotlessness. They are our mothers and sisters and wives that we pledge to protect and love. The sisters. What we to them and they to us, will be the definition of our nation to be.

The children must be taught by us.
The wives must be taught by us.
Ourselves must be taught by us. This is the way to love as a nation
of strength.
All this that we see is our nation at the bateye of momentary pause here in the West. The angel in charge stares at us, and begs in the heart of change for us to go in the right direction. Bismillah, Rahman, Rahim, Humdulilah, Rabil ala min. This beams through voidness. This sings through blank ness. White
ness.
We must raise ourselves. O holy people.

In our terr bul ness

We meet, sister, in a form, in a place, too much for us. Each path

will lead thru the self.

The thing we want to reach. The triumph of a way of life. A

Way of feeling. They on the street looking past each other to

they own self.

Not just to love, but to be love, itself.

What Trane and the many

other black teachers Mwalimu spoke of. Love Supreme. So the act of

communication, is faith. (Karenga is the master teacher. Maulana.)

So the feather man and his soft yaller woman. have met love. He

speaking earth magic air magic actual grace in her ear. The look.

The blood need to be told as hiply and as gently, else somebody

have to beat his ass.

But we cd move perhaps from here. Meeting you on the street,

with all our lives floating inside our eyes. A smile. A tenuous

touching of you love. We are love, our self. I love you babee,

you touch what beauty is, and make me with

your touch,

so beautiful

hold me, yeh

make me

beautiful.

Not the special occasion. (That Smokey Robinson sings of.)

But

the day

to day

always

continuous exercise

of

astonishing grace.

Some ter—bul dudes. The glimpse of reality. Not simple fact, which

is the object trying to talk. But truth. The settling beneath

appearance to what is shining like the hot beautiful holy sun.

So the blood. Whatever we say. Always talk so bad about the blood.

"The blood aint ready. A nigger aint shit. Negroes aint got no

values. Man, these spooks'll make you tired, with they shit." And

on and on. Trapping ourselves in screens of negative description.

When we know we bad. Shit, we here. We here and gonna survive.

PRAYER FOR SAVING

Survive and Defend.

Survive and Defend.

Defend the space you live upon Defend your family your way of

     feeling

     about the world. Defend The Impressions

     and Muhammad Ali

     Defend Ray Robinson and the Songhay Empires

     Defend the Pyramids and Huey Newton in the same breath the same

     people faced with the same disasters in the physical world, the

emergence of the naked apes on horseback from out the icebox zones

the squares with paper ears and wooden steps against whom we must defend

inspite of whom we must survive

defend and survive

let black green and red survive, and the angle of success, pyramid

let moses appear and be chastised in our songs

for sleeping around and talking too much

like Broad street's liberal niggers

let our words and music survive

let the temptations please let their feeling survive

Please Black People Defend John Coltrane and SunRa

Claude McKay must survive his long black knowledge walks

in footprint sands of europe america and west indies must stand

his banana boats and homes in harlem must be protected at all costs

and Duke Ellington we must hear him in the 22nd century as

sweetly and the flying images of sound enlightenment his

diminuendos and crescendos must be preserved behind the alleyways and broken

stoops of Howard Street and Centre Street and all the Wattses and

Houghs must be protected with Duke there and the Vandellas

recoloring everything in our reach. We must paint these falling

buildings brilliant moorish arabesques of Ankhs and

riming love words of Egyptian light and reunderstand that death

is not horrible but merely graduation if we are together into a new

adventure, in our more spiritual forms

    Defend the way you walk my man sister tell him to do it

    the coolness like we really meant by cool slow fire protect

let it survive as the universal oasis of civilization. Build new

blackbeautiful things. New Shapes

    Buildings · · · · ·

               l
                i

           k   hi
          e   t   s "WILD" STUFF
                ECSTASY HAPPENINGS

                   sun comes up on a street like kisses

survive to do your real thing

defend the energy the hipness in you

it is too valuable that people everywhere understand

why we got so many dances

why we like colors

why we able to run so fast and fight so hard

why jimmy brown cd carry six dudes on his back for forty yards

and beat five outta his way

this must rise all of it, jimmies runs must televise movie

reality in fast and slow motion for ever till change makes it new

jimmy name amunubi rakaptah or some future black rich swiftness

like it, city

must mean 40 yards beatin dudes off him

music must have ground crushed sun walls

screams in the woodwork in orange and blue

mayor must mean big black holy man

must mean again, a prince

blessed with the wisdom of a strong people

    Survive

    and Defend

    Survive

    and Defend

suedes and maroon pants

warm breeze over some kinda other brown

in the bed listening to each other breathe

those smiles of

our women and giggles of

our running children

their brilliant drinkknowledge eyes

    Survive

and Defend. Draw around fight to the end

   The end of Square Worship

   and Ugliness. The end of

   Corniness, and meat selfishness

 Survive

and Defend all these things in us

All These Things We are

Or Come From

  Defend Defend Survive and Defend

   Spirit of Black Life

   Live In Immortality

   For

   Ever

But look at it. We were brought here slaves and survived that. Now we are trying literally to get our selves back together. Meanwhile we have a substance from king priestly magic that remains even with us in icebox land. This is the bright gold of our image here. No matter. Spirit. No matter all the heavy "fact" of our being here like dis. Shit. Man, dont mess wit me. Checking out the every body.

Consciousness is what we need. It is all that will bring us back to ourselves

But we must organize and be in organization. An organization (FOI here

from the mosque) is the swell of next level consciousness.

Bigger than the individual. We move from the single to the many

to the larger the city, the nation. And then past there we move

to many nations, as one, as Nkrumah and Garvey envision, the many

blacks into the One Huge Black Nation, strong as the divinity in

us.

The brothers sit here doing it this way. One day it will be one way.

Allah will be on everybodys mind . . no matter what they call it. And

then one day, everybody will even call it the same thing. And what's

so beautiful in life will be for and before everybody and we will all, all

the humans, have evolved to walk through life beautiful more than

anything.

The theme of this is the together revelation of humanhood.

The journey is funny.

You got the money in your heart

to make it

man a man's gonna make it the way he got to do

you can come on baby

and walk with me

I'm gonna do all the things allah want me to

LECTURE PAST DEAD CATS

(Scatter energy little holes too small to be what should be)

    what should be is

    what we gonna do

    how we gonna move

    in the right direction

O nation of super hip swift motional creation

O people of natural sweet smoothness

O Beings of the double clutch

    the attitude

    the slide

    the fake

    the stuff

    the slow hang in the air

O delicate vibratories of ecstatic madness shimmering

in falsetto worship spires of cool goodness

O tone carriers of glowing magic

G
E
S
T
U
R
E

of sudden stops

and jiggles

O spangle of cosmic prepostelectronic color

Black mohair spirits

Evolutional saviours of the worth of humanity

(if it is to be considered as worthy of divinity)

O nearest interpreters of divinity and regality

O beautiful sounds of the existent

It is an honor to be one of your priests

Let us commune in our hooked up downess, our consumate bad ness

as together specimens

of laughing magic

Let us gesture the invisible symbols of constant creation

HEY HEY HEY !!!

It is an honor to be one of the priests

One of the blessed.

Teach

Imamu Baraka

Not cuteness but realness

                              (the new consciousness

Not pieceness but wholeness

reveald nation

revealed truth that makes you laugh a burr

softness welled in the sound

i dig the way this dude walk dont you

The blood is the nation in its entirety. What's pictured here is

our nation.

Like this blood with the tooth pick. Can you put a kafiyah on him

where he stands. Mchawi a wizard they could all be wizards. They

could and are. The toothpick spraying it around. The touch of light.

Transformed wood. A wand. Transmutation. The dumb wood now

vibrating at a higher rate. With the blood. His mouth wand.

The toothpick of the blood is his casual swagger stick. Sho

is hip.

Catches the light

in the steel town

catches a dancers

eye. A smile like a city

laugh

years later

of hard

sunlight

(Hey whydo youse carry that in your mout' Kookiefangblood asked)

This is the core. The music under the skin. Of the blood. The way

we walk is a relation to our majesty. The way we hump under shadders.

The blood. Worship us because we close to god. This man got a tooth

pick. Yeh. Can you dig it??

Triangle and leader.

Down peacocks. Be down. Whey they move for all of us as pretty.

With the banner of our nation flying up a pole in our heads. Like

that easy and swift. the heart of our being is the blood. Our street

image. The all over known. Not Ralph Bunche. (John Coltrane is a spirit

hovering over us. James Brown is a spirit changing our bodies

to light.) But the blood here. The colored bodys themselves a

truth of what is and what will be. You been in a rechange. A

riot. A rebellion. Chains go. Chairs gone. TV in color a load

a drugs. Carry you ass out you in the way. One day they will move

for all of us like they used to. Carrying our banner. Chaka.

Samory. Pianki. One day, one night they will move in something

too loud to be on losers, like this down streets and evil will

just be something dull.

Babee everything's all right

Up Tight

Outta sight.

I wanted to put the image of real life. Of the new rulers of the world before all eyes. Roy Wilkins is a dumb slave. The future rulers are black

ALL IN THE STREET

Can you imagine something other
than what you
see Something
Big Big & Black
Purple yellow
Red & green (but Big, Big & Black)
Something look like a city
like a Sun Island gold-noon
Flame emptied out of heaven
grown swollen in the center
of the earth
Can you imagine who would live
there
with gold streets
striped circled inlaid
with pageants of the rulers
victories . . . Imagine these streets
along which walk some people
some evolved humans
look like *you*

maybe walk, stroll
rap like you
but maybe a lil difference
maybe different clothes
hip mighta changed
a lil, but they shoes still glow
black and brown mirrors for things
in the street
to dig themselves
mounds of round sounds bubblin and bumpin
right out the ground
can dig it . . . uh?
can see it . . . uh?
can feel it . . . uh?
can be it . . . huh?
This is now-past what you touch today
can change black man behaving under
your touch the way you want it to.
Can you digit . . . uh?
See, feel, touch, be
it, uh?

The homes like domes high sparkling pyramids

New red sphinx buildings, cat buildings

Sun buildings, star buildings, the teaching

of invisible beings . . . Who we are is

THE MAGIC PEOPLE . . . the Black Genius

Prophets of the Planet . . . Look at

the clothes on the women the

beautiful sisters clothed in supernew

silk looking spun diamond lace

the geles and bubas of a future generation

as they sail across the city on their

way out rugs . . . way out waaaaay

out way out, past the disease

of the cracker ruled present, when

We are men and women again

freed from the serpent's dung

Hear each other miles apart

(Without no telephones)

"Love I hear you from way cross the

sea . . . in East Africa . . . Arabia . . .

Reconstructing the grace of our

long past I hear you love

whisper at the soft air as it bathes

you—I hear and see you"

"I hear and see you too brother jones

from the year 1968 talking to me,

My long departed ancestor

The sounds and images are here where

you left them. All for us"

Time space manifest into the unity of

the creator, The Creator has all experiences

and we live as flying images of

endless imagination. Listen to the creator

speak in me now. Listen, these words

are part of God's thing. I am a

vessel, a black priest interpreting

the present and future for my people
Olorun—Allah speaks in and
thru me now . . . He begs me to
pray for you-as I am doing-He
bids me have you submit to
the energy.

He bids me pray that you submit
to the energy . . . the energy the energy the energy

The energy the energy the energy the rays
of God roared thru us all . . . uh
rays of God plunged thru us all-uh
bids me raise myself to tell you
Look!
Listen!
I am in an ecstasy a swoon in
actual touch with everything

These future rulers
are black
I see & hear them
now
I am in touch
with them. They speak and
beckon to me
Listen they speak thru
my mouth

"Come on—
Come on—
Come on—
Come on—
Come on—
Come on—"
They are in the energy
they have created, through their consciousness
a closer connection
with the energy

They speak thru
my mouth
"Come on—
Come on—
Come on—
Come on—
Come on—
Come on—"

On their way out rugs in silken garments

no cold can penetrate

They speak and beckon at you all

Thru me now, as ancestors

We are the ancestors of

these black builders

and conquerors

They would appear right here to

say these things but do not want to

frighten you

instead

they speak thru

me

they say—"All Praise Black Fathers

and Mothers We Know the Struggle

you go thru now

We know how hard it is to be black

in that primitive age But do not

naaw . . . do not ever despair

We Won

We Here

We Still fast and grooving

We Still baddest thing on the planet

We Still gentle hummers and obeeda scatters

OObbbeeoobbee dah
oobbbeeoobbee dah

dah

dah

daaaaah daaah oobbie obbie dah

Do not despair Ancient People
We are your children
and We have conquered
This is your blessing
and this is your reward
Do not despair gentle ancient
groovy ancestors.
We have conquered
and we await the rich legacy
of hard won blackness
which you create to leave
us
here in the black fast future
here among the spiritual creations
of natural man
Do not despair ancient fathers and
Mothers there in old America
We are here
awaiting your gorgeous
Legacy . . . . ."

Here the contact is broken · · · · ·

Imamu Amiri Baraka

A do rag. What can you do

Can you do

the thing

most any

fling a brick through

the devils

eyes

Good God I'm black and fast as life itself.

(pointing in dark. At YOU)

The reason we stress race and culture, is the fact of these categories dominance in the affairs of men. All activity is cultural activity. A church is a smile. The cooking of food, a walk is as profound as a system of judging. A walk, there half lit by stars pointing nex tu my man, is a judgement there, in the midst of, Life as refiner and definer. So each act is the total. And if you can see you can see this. Bad breath is a bad idea. Simply. What is issued, what is shown, by anything, is its definition.

So there in the dark pointing at you. The pointer and the pointed at both have substance vibrating meaning. The Waltz is specific. The Boogaloo is specific. Charlie Chaplin and Daly are the Pope and Mozart, just as James Brown, and my brothers sliding through the dark are Chaka and Amenotep. God is all styles.
I hate to use the word, God. God is all styles, together.
His style is all styles. But each of us is a vector carrying meaning.

Terribleness is a definition. It
is a description. Muhammad Ali is a terrible dude. You member
when he beat Chuvalo's ass. Kept stickin his hand in the sucker's
face. Yeh. Man thass a terrible dude. For real.

But it is commoner than that. All
our terribleness is our total. Our hipness is in anything we touch.
(Wow the weatherman's talking like a nigger. Damn the MC sound like
a junkie. Uptight? What? Aw man you dont even know what the fuck
up tight mean. You need your head tighten 'swhat you need . .

YEH. WOW.

The sitting there like that is us deep too. All of us.

This is a certain approach to everything. Abernatheeeeee. This

dude. Man. He walking in the street and shit. Bang. Dude gotta

shot. Like right off. And the music of the blade. Shoodoooo.

Keep it. Against the leather and suede of us. The hat of us.

The pulled backness and alligatorness (meaning black in the

hieroglyph this alligator back you got on your feets my ming).

What you gonna call it. Like a cracker sit on a bench jump up

and down saying why you guise always palay fancy. Fancy? Fancy?

Fantasy. For them. Are we giants, we Ethiopians! For sure. You

remember man they used to call us giants named their gods after

our warriors.

Yes my man we play fancy. Everything we do we do fancy. We, r

selves, are fancy. Fancy Dudes. Bloods. Slick Fast Bad ass Bloods.

We glisten in black leather.

Drums hammer the streets of america its bloods' walkin. Talkin

about Florsheims! What we want is to have Willie Waller's hip

shoes from the ground up.

Might have lights on the motherfuckers.

Thats what the knives are for. Jive asses on their way to Belly

Bottle a martini suburb with prefucked wife soup as a television

game called swap god and see death as cool. Naw we want life.

BIG

The hand, one arm

or leg

stiff

drug. (lil ol greylady asked me if i was cripple

i said yeh, i hurt my leg

but her eye was

cripple man

i was

cool

The institutions will conduct the electricity will contain it

for our purpose. So that what is cripple will in reality for feeding

us be COOL. And the uncool the cripple eye the paper ear will

be forced to their own (?) resources, and we can fly with ours.

The attitude man. Baraka, man. (Japanese/Yugen) yeh, like he do,

JB, shaking in one place. The attitude. In the midst of

all

the one focus of energy. The

      Grace.

— Badada Badada Badada

  Badada Badada Badada aaa —

The way people act is the way they act in all things. The Big and The Small, only the magnitude, not the style. John Coltrane must rule us. That sensibility. Blood winding through night beating sticks together must rule us. That consciousness. Dudes that can hang in the air, double up, stuff!! or hold one arm stiff turning the corner Abernathy said "Bop do be do be dillia do be da da do be dopp woo daaaaa" If you can dig it. This is our expression. This is the change. And even the language the words will change. And the meaning will be manifest.

This is our leadership

this is our kingdom to come

as it comes out of our hearts

to find strength in the common world.

We will raise it and develop it

and certainly defend it.

(on the stoops)

And this is the common man he standin on the stoops waiting for

the world to turn (on) for the cycle to come full out for the devil

to die and the angels to live. We all waitin.

But it will be a value system

that changes us. Something that preaches Unity, Self Determination,

Collective Responsibility, Collective Economics, Purpose, Creativity,

and Faith.* Faith in Blackness. Changes us to Powerful Beings on the

planet. Our style will remain. The buildings will scream at heaven

as they rise the spires of the tranemind the pyramids of the sunra

mind the endless scatting of yusef rahmanesques to the towers of new

light for the black cities to be.

*(NGUZOSABA, 7 Principles of US Organization, MAULANA KARENGA, Founder Chairman)

We understand the cycle now.

We must ready ourselves for the power to come. The devil done played

out. We must make ourselves ready to assume control of our own destiny.

As the majority of the world's people must ready themselves too.

Like the old people said about the sun shinin on our back door . . .

add the front my man, for sure, the front too.

Simply that one way of life will

pass. Like any man's life. From babyhood to middleage to death.

(Change.) And the west will pass, and we who are the slaves will

take control. Let it be the beauty in us that takes control. Let

it be even longer than 5000 years that we rule this time.

The scientists must show us the way to survive the endless cycle

of back and forth. The pendulum of rise and fall. The Religious

Scientists.

We are fighting now that

Religion and Science finally be seen as one thing. And that all

thought is holy and factual, at the same time.

We are fighting for the change, to survive into the new epoch.

And what the change will be is in us. It is indicated already,

by who we are. The Muslims will tell you that Islam was to be

brought to the West. It has been brought. So the rule of the

wise will eventually be brought to the West. The Wise. The Sable

Heads, of the wise. The Wool Men.

> (So The Magi, under the for rent
>
> sign)

The dude in the middle is the leader. Always. Can you dig it. And

our leader. That temper will rise. Is Risen. (Everything round here's

for rent. But not for money, in the final, the money will die and

rent will be older than these houses and space, finally, is free,

as we will be. FREE.

All the cities are for rent.

We will rent them to ourselves.) That Leader Will Lead. He will lead

us. That touch and taste . . . fly thru the air . . . dip . . . uhhh . . . wit

you bad sef . . . will come to pass to point and grin . . . digit from the

top . . . the clean air of black reason a spiral through planet sun . . .

to pass to point and grin at subjects and objects as master of its

own space. Institutional space and territorial space. We are in our

kingdoms already. We are our culture. Let us bring ourselves to power

Brothers ! ! !

Let us bring our ancient culture to mastery once again.

ANSWERS IN PROGRESS

Walk through life
beautiful more than anything
stand in the sunlight
walk through life
love all the things
that make you strong, be lovers, be anything
for all the people of
earth.

You have brothers
you love each other, change up
and look at the world
now, its
ours, take it slow
we've a long time, a long way
to go,

We have
each other, and the
world,
dont be sorry
walk on out through sunlight life, and know
we're on the go
for love
to open
our lives
to walk
tastin the sunshine
of life.

A Sun Being

"Adoration of Ra when riseth he in horizon eastern of heaven."

The eating of sun streams. Fly soul (Het Ba) from his temple.
The unleashed. Not a ball but the raging sky of fire. Hot souls
such as ours the unimagined ecstasy of my childhood sometimes.
What the thrust to completion is was in me and thrilled me so
much. It shook me out of earth. The legends of my imagination.
I flew. I winged thru space man fine and clean. The rays of my
electric skullbrain mind illuminated the way I traveled. And I
looked at things and marveled at their color and movement.
At their speech, so deep and profound it was. Symbols. Red crane
like birds. A staff. A cross with a man's head. I made some signs
with my hands. Little boy. I was laughing the feeling was the flight
itself. The laughter powered me.

All this I know to be in us. All this opening to brighter feeling.

New Reality. Not dream, not frustrated illusion. But new reality

from new consciousness. New only because we are stuck in brown knotty

wood extricated only by the will to be. We must exist as sunbeings

the laughter in our shoes. Man it tickles you to think about that

dont it? I dont care about no thing. Its laughter. As pure divinity

could only be pure laughter, and speed. Bright Things swing higher

than the low touches of the pendulum.

RUN FREE FREE SPIRIT RUN FREE

Can you make sense at top speed. Go faster. This is a race being
told by itself to do this. Go Faster. GO FASTER. Creation at the
top of the game. BE BE BE BE BE BE BE BE BE BE BE BE BE BE BE
BE BE BE B EEEEEEE as passes and (things?) were. And ever are.

The key is to lift above the cycle. What was will be. But reality
remains the same beneath *seemingly* endless illusion. Only reality
is endless.

PEACE IN PLACE

TIME AFTER TIME AFTER TIME AFTER TIME
AFTER TIME
AFTER TIME
AFTER TIME AFTER TIME AFTER TIME A LIE
TIME A LIE

THE SUN IS THE BEING OF FIRE AND HEAT
ALL ENERGY COMES FROM THE SUN
SUN OF GOD
SOULS OF GODFUL SUNS
SONS OF THE DEEPNESS IN US
DEEPNESS OF ALL BEING ALL THE BEING ALL OF THE FOREVER ALL OF THE SPACE
I AM USING ALL OF THE SPACE ALL OF THE SPACE FILL THE SPACE ALL THE
SPACE MY VOICE IS NOT HEARD MY FLESH IS NOT SEEN IT IS ALL THE SAME
FLESHVOICEHEATRAY ALL THE SAME HOTCHOICE ALL THE FIRELIFE COMING
COMING ALL SUN COMING FIRE COMING BEING COMING SPURTINGS DRIBBLINGS
SPARKLINGS CRYINGS BELLING CHIMING CRYING SPACKLECRACKLEING
WHINING BEINGS HIGH BEINGS A BEING ONE BEING A SUN A SUN BURNING
WORSHIP THE ALL-MIGHTY SUN. THE SUN IS OUR GOD THE SUN IS THE GOD
THE SUN IS THE WORSHIPER HIMSELF.

I am the son . . . . . yahaaa ooooo yahaaaoooo deedeedeedee come ba cho
I am the son the black holiness the goodness yaaaahoooo yaaaaaaaaaaa
Wake me up in me seeing you you son you touch the goldeness yaaaaahoooo
Yaaaahoooooo sun in me rising above the tininess the space is filled
listen to son burn through you burn you up burn you up burn you up
yaaaaaaa dir dir rummmmmm rummmmmm doo eee dooo eee doooo eeeee gooooo

Worshiping the sun a brother makes these sounds this is the self
that points to nothing points to itself being hot
eyes of fire warm me
Listen to the brother yahhhhoooooeeeeeeeayayayayayayaya
The black brother doing his thing, Ima do my thing always
I'ma always do my thing who dont like it, you dont like it foooooo
dododod foooo dont get together run a slackjoke crate. Didn't know
it was weusi apollo last sun being first sun being in ghana in a gold
benny heatin up magic to reuse space better. Ima do my space using
thing now, watch out cold stuff, heatin up heatin up look at him
can you diiiiiiiiiiiiiiiiigg it?? can you diiiiiiiiiiiiiiggggit can you
use space this way cracker, naw you cant, where's jb come out do yo
dance clean up space, watch out for that motherfuckin flag dude, can
you diiiiiiiiiiiiweusi apollo thales inventin sidespace . . . beepadeep
in space creatin new waves sidespace inside a drop of enrgy creatin
being the energy the creator the lion man the dancer

groodasa bam bam crazy jump a dooby the rammer cut him cut out
icame back bleedin cape and shit hammer and shit horse and shit
standin in the san a natural man bad as bad could be ima bad dude
anyway see my gold hat and hundred books and a stable of dudes spell
any shit you want bam bam bam bam slook at weusi mchoro allah be
praised he dance. look clean up space clean up bam worshiping the
heavy self of fire. worshiping the heavy being of warmth and light.

AFTER A LIE TIME
AFTER A TIME, A LIE
AFTER LYING TIMING LIFETIME AFTER ALLL TIME IS A LIE
LIE AFTER TIME GO AFTER TIME LIE LIE IN TIME LYING
THERE IS WORK TO DO DO YOU SEE IT DO YOU KNOW HOW MUCH WORK
THERE IS TO DO
TO WORK TO WORK THERE IS AFTER TIME WORK AFTER LIES WORK
WILL YOU WORK PAST TIME WILL YOU LIE PAST WORK OR WORK OR WORK REAL
WORK REAL WORK BEATS LIE TIME TIME LIES DEAD WORK CAN
WORKING IN TIME
WORKING ALL THE TIME
WORKING THROUGH TIME, PAST IT. DEAL WITH THE GREAT ENSIDERGEE
FIREFINGERS...GOLDSPARKS...ELECTRIC HAIR...EYEBURSTS...CRACKLE
SPACKLE EYEBURSTS...FIREFINGERS
NET GOD SPREAD BURSTS FIREFINGERS THREADHEAT PUNCTURE
HOTPUNCTURES
HOTPUNCTURES
HOTPUNCTURES
HOTPUNCTURES ARE EYEBURSTS AND FIREFINGERS
CRACKLESPACKLE EYEBURSTS ARE FIREFINGERS...DEADTIME...NO IMAGE
CRAKKKK CRAKK CRAKK CRAKK CRAKK
CRACKLESPACKLE HOTPUNCTURE SPREADBURST
EYE TIME BUILDS PAST LIE
HOTPUNCTURES DRIES TO PYRAMID (silverimage of the sun
sparkleing chrome image of the sungod

```
      P
        L
          A
            C
              E
                  O
                    F
                        P
                          E
                            A
                              C
                                E
```

WORSHIP THE SUN IN TIME
WORSHIP THE SUN OUTSIDE TIME
WORSHIP THE SUN WITH NO TIME
WORSHIP THE TIMELESS SUN
THE SUN IS THE BEING OF FIRE AND HEAT
THE SUN IS THE CHANGER OF ENERGIES
THE SUN IS THE GOLDEN MUSIC
THE SUN IS BRIGHT HOT AND FREE
THE SUN BURNS US BLACK AND GORGEOUS FOREVER
THE SUN IS OURSELVES THE SUN IS OUR SELVES THE SUN IS OUR
SOULFUL BLACK SELVES.

So it is that each sensibility has its own ultimate concerns.

Its own seeming reality. But we must make something that duplicates,

that is the reality itself. Each inch is adventure. All direction

included. The whole of evolution in consciousness. To master the

lower laws with higher laws. To make ourselves extensions of those

higher laws.

Picture ourselves as free rulers of all (our) space. You see value

systems are "god". The adherence to them, the prayer, the supplication,

the living by the rule of, &c., strength. So the various Romes,

white or black, like the pulpy fruit, devoid of creativity. So the

spectators at our national pastimes proball or riots, pulpy, devoid

of creativity. Lost from God. In with, in fact they are, the debil.

But the robes, man, and them white skies and black skies, them

flowers MOTHERS DAY, all the mothers days of our various lives.

To lay against the intricacies of the human spirit with flesh judging

ourselves by our very attire and attitude. It is god judging us.

By the way we are. The circle if you see it. That the existent exists

as a judgment of its own energy, and in the way of its disposition

is its "decision" its definition, of itself.

So Cool is Cool. &c. Evil, evil, from the biggest of all mouths,

said, finally, and forevermore eternally.

was there was there was burning burn
ooooo came back see your mouth working
work out work out
slid got up from splittin split for days
here come beauty beauty here come beauty
here go here go look dig
yehhhh
yehhhh
worshiping the sun the sun
the fire worship the fire
worship the fire
the invisible always burning fire
the invisible always burning fire
the cracklespackle firebursts thunder lighting niggers
worship niggers

worship niggers
niggers should worship suns should worship the heat of blackness
as it turns you soul it turns you black its black beatin heat out
you heatin up the world
heat up you heatin heat up you heatin heat up heat heat heat
nigger worshiping blackness is blackness
space blackness waaaayyyyy dig it dig it yeh
waayyyyyy space blackness nigger worship space sun is god
sun is god waaayyyyyyy space blackness
blackness
blackness
blackness
blackness
blackness
blackness

                    yeaaaaaaaaaaaaaaaaaaaaaaaaa's god

/The picture of Jawbones and Paul is perfection more than any
image i've seen. (Can you understand that the body is alive?
Khan said everything aspires to humanity. Human form. Even the
body itself. As part of itself. The two male tits and navel and
the penis are a big face. Talk coming out of the joint. That is
that kinda talk. Just as the hole in the head gives head talk./

The faces collect the change. They are the culture. (And Maulana's definitions for a "criteria" for a culture, can be traced right back behind that face, as to what it contains, from where, and to what ends?) It is all part of our Mythology, and our pursuits were and will be again formal religion, tho when the actual truth is told out the thing will die if its just about form. Khan says "Death is the tax the soul has to pay for having a name or a form". So it must not be about forms. We had forms, for our set, then. As there are forms now, negative forms, the other pole, we find our place as now. So in the future there will be new forms to contain our holy energy.

Mythology History Social Organization Political Organization Economic Organization Creative Motif and Ethos, these Maulana teaches us are the criteria, for a culture. And the definition of just where that culture's at, is easy to dig for the digger.

The path of the peoples.
The Whole Body:

Children
Dudes
Bloods
Sisters
Old People (Ol Folks)
Roots

In our history we must teach what bloods were and why they doin what they doin here in the icebox now. na. My man with the ear ring understands in his finger tips and the energy whisper struts through his body understands. And this is what the ancient brothers had discovered and tried to isolate. The power to survive.
The lesson of the mummies. The vulgarity of one form is the lesson of the whole.

It is your spirit man that survives and if it is strong as the god-system you are as cause then the effect will be closeness to divinity the first cause the ultimate reality,

My man here with the black pirate do rag, the earring, the penetrating eyerays and hat on backwards to defeat all dis couraging talk about who's where doing what. The hat is bad. 'sa bad sky you got on my man. A Bad Sky??? The ethos. The drench of directives teaching us to be opposite devil at all cost. Except the bought who are slow-joe the tied up in the neck, sucking breath from pollution. Crimes against nature determine the brevity of society. Fish belly up. Niggers, quiet as its kept, are part of nature.

An ethos, an ethic. A soul value. A determinant of path. Road Runner to the region of refinement. Just as bloods in fantastic robes once looked at caveswine wondering what on earth that shit could possibly be, so we do this now, my man, in one sense, but at our selves, in another sense, and the only salvation will be our selves, through an ethical system that speaks from, out of, because of and to, our higher selves. *The Spirit Reach.*

All the criteria are present, because we, ourselves, are present.

And have been present. It is just the focus must return, the energy

must be redirected. The energy must be harnessed, so that

our forms will be given power. Will be EMPOW

ERED

POW

ER

POW!!!

WUHER......

The energy is random all possibility in creation precreation except

the ever existent. The will, the male principle, the direction, the

being to the becoming, (the female). The creation, then, of form(**S**).

And with the form, the cycle of life. We can not escape the natural

cycle but we can counterbalance the negative effects, yes, man, we can,

by *becoming positive causes*.

All styles are epochs. They come again and agin. What is was, and

so forth.

Man.

But we are to be conscious to retaste as a form and institution.

The spirit of the stiff leg or the screaming horn will be in the

institutions we build. When that is freed from material to reinvent

material it can be healthy and grow for a time in, it is then that the

brother with his hand jammed down in his pocket like that will look out

calmly across all the field of beauty he had made

> (Ra-ist melody of sunlight
> in two hundred years
> a children's anthem

Is it about Economics? Yesssssssssss definitely, my man. (This

was a dude in a leather jacket with a icecube on his knee. The

blood with the bad sky was askin him what he meant he talked about

a dude with a Trot Sky. A what kinda sky? (Cruse be cool man! We

heard you!) He was trying to explain about Marx or no it was about

a bullet slammin through his stomach he fell heavily and the crackers

wore black and dug it the tears were so heavy not that for us, man,

not that again. A black ideology please. A measure of our selves,

to be our selves. Please dont go for the iceman dressed as Palm Beach

Pat the beard wearing saviour of the subject peoples. Race and

Culture determine the world. Politics is a subbranch as definition

of ACTIVITY within the total. Marxism is white political thought.

Where translated as Mao or Nkrumah, or Ho, it is Maoism or Nkrumahism

or Hoism, but not Europa, except as it fails to be adequate.

(*Voice From Conakry* or Mao on Krush, &c.)

It's about all activities within the whole. But Culture, the

totality of all activities, is the whole. Hence the Seven Criteria.

But it is just that the substance of reality, the vector from the

absolute, that we are (brother with the pirate set) determines

itself by its closeness to itself. And that all of existence is this

same "journey," or heartbeat. But we are, as Lionel Hampton used to

say, Flyin Home.

Sure the blood is creative. He is the creator, no doubt. dude

his hand jammed down one leg out front and a cap them other dudes

at random the one in the middle's the leader man!

Remember The Toilet a play by LeRoi Jones? Never seen nobody

standin in fronta the Public Barber Shop. Our humanity is

determined by our consciousness of it. The devil can only say

how quaint as he sets you up for the ice. Or how bad and hateful.

((as he sets you up for the ice. Or ignore you, man, walk away

while you got ts eliot socks around yr ears singing three blind

mice and they your step n fechit philosophers the wisest on the

planet. "Shiiiit Iaint doin nuthin...."

So the criteria, the already existent, must be refocused,

changed to reflect the absolute. The Unity, which is the reality.

"The closer we come to unity, (Umoja) the closer we get to reality."

They are the same.

The dude with his hand in his pocket in healthy black mythology.

Priest in the religion, a conductor of the energy, not a secret god hisself,

but a conductor of the energy. Just as we all are. And more so when

we CONSCIOUS. Just as these images here, conductors of the energy.

And all of the energy that each of these images is, (not represents, but *is*)

conscious of itself as together as vectors of the absolute, at that moment

is the absolute will. Represents it. Social Economic Political Creative, all

as vectors of the one Being. Us, we talking about. Must be focused through.

We speak of our traditional greatness. It is the code that made us great. The natural qualities given strength by the purity of their essence as our concerns. 42nd Street is part of a man, part of his brain. Nixon and the hippies are part of a brain, igniting substances in the grey ethereal definition of a "race." The bullets wing into John Kennedy's throat. Crackers dreamed this themselves being themselves rising falling without space or time poof poof in them beings the changes the odors the screams and murders. Poof poof in them beings, like America is a being like Rome was a being like Atlantis was a being. Fish belly up.

Stanin here wit ma brother, is all of it i need to know here. It'll be

all right.

Cain' ge kill

gonna be

all

right

you gotta nigul

I gotta dime, way out in the woods with a flyin snake

S'funny what all this means. What these images mean. I wanted you

to see the Blood. I wanted you Blood to see you, swiftest man.

What is natural and existent can be focused using the best as

reference thru the value system, the attention to, blackness.

So social organization exists how does it exist, and how must

it exist to strengthen? It is communal. It is, as the economic

tone is communal, but it the communal tho it already exists

must be taught to us again, must be brought to light. It must

be re presented to our consciousness again, so that it is tight as

a supportive muscle must be.

Same blood. But the unity. Beneath illusion. That somehow this dude with the bike or this dude with the stripey robe is different from the funny dude with the chain or my man jawbones. Beneath illusion is reality. Unity. Digit. Sit for the service. Pay attention to the preacher. Yeh. Now.

We cd look into the future

on brooooome street mister

stanin w

mabrother

i's all

i need to know.

Sblam!

(More to come))

See all of it again. See yrself again. You need power, man.
You need to be ruling something. Lookin in the door with the
light eyes the fire eyes the perfect lips you need to be in
charge of somethin, like yrself. I can take off these clothes
and wear some others. I can unchain air held to a stone be
myself gettin up! I can scrape my brain of poison fat and keep
from gettin sclerosis of the medulla, or brain fever or
scholarshipism. A nigger w/a coke in his hand (how the "middleclass"
blood fails) or w/some jammed up his nose (how the other one
get took off) bloods together nonethe less dig it dig it.

Draw away from the diseased body ... STEP 1

Embrace the blackness, the alternative ... STEP 2

(From there the seven principles) and the creation of the nation where

we stand.

"DAZED AND OUT OF THEIR WOOL HEADS..."

the conquered, the prisoners, stand in line
to watch what they're ordered to watch, it could be
the moon, the evilest of selves, the pretender to light like
the master of artificial science himself, the synthesizer, himself
synthesized, a synthesis, a sin thesis, of all the negative elements
all the opposites possible in creation. You have moon-man, the cracker.
Whom the dazed and conquered submit to every day. Beneath their own gaze
beneath the gaze of their own God, they still submit to moonman. They
act like moonman, look like they think moonman look, talk like moonman,
lo and behold they will stand up in front of moonman and tell moonman they
hate him, when it is moonman with his jaded lacklight self completing the
sentence with heavy stick infested breathing, being his own kicks and kick
er moonman moonmaid moonteeth pronged through living breathing young
animals dazed animals drugged animals duped animals animals with contracts
animals licking on other animals involved with the graceless killer reflect
of their own potential eminence because they will not emanate from themselves
but use the killer darts the sticks the iron bars sunk in moonmans eyes
as their lighting, when the heavens are full of legitimate lightning

when the prisoners heads are full of electrical vibrations jumping right
out of they wool thick skies. The moon has them hypnotized. Watching the
killer beings emerge cloaked in bloodthoughts and maniacal whines, beneath
themselves as emanations from themselves, the beastly moon eat up their
eyes mess up their skies, twists the prisoners blackfeeling minds
the moon
lies
in the heavens
it is only a beatle
imitating
Otis Redding (an insect trying to be a man)
Oh my dazed and imprisoned brothers
Sunpeople out of whose insides all warmth and light are created
Be your selves Be your self all selves into that big burning
Holy One
Make it bright day for us all, so we can see better and be warm and happy
Be your self again, Son, Light up this dark old world

Imamu

We say race and culture, and the images, these pictures, identify a race and a culture. You see what we want is that everything be totally fulfilled as a being of consciousness. If you cannot understand this then you should be in training.

I cant say more than that except all the visions and thoughts you've had actually exist. I want you to have the strength and power to achieve these in our reality. The reason religion preaches "goodness" is because this is the backbone, the projection necessary to move in the direction of realization and understanding. Life itself is perfection the closer you are to its essence the closer you are to immortality and total realization.

                              and find ourselves pointed at by

shotguns, or the events not here yet. It would glisten in

our eyes in the shadows. You need to be sitting somewhere

with yr arm around yr main man and some black cherry soda

Mr. Florsheim king. When he get a shoe factory willie waller

from howard street shoes might have lights on the motherfuckers

(you *said* that, but can you *do*

it

Fly

You dig metal or space. be space space *is* flight. You see air

planes are not the final word on flying, nor is lincoln center

the final word on whats its spose to be the finally word on

huntington? These tombs are not our buildings. Them dudes with the cherry coke is not interested in no windowless bullshit

like you goin for CheapCharles the Howard Graduate, postfacto

proxyism he got from his master the iceman who we tryin to see

goeth straight on out. James slid right out from unnerneath

the camera. Dude had some cleanclothes on his knee.

Got from them censored he censored. Clean clothes out. The Sheims,

and, unfortunately, some dope. Thas cheapecharlie's recycle

of wealth back to his machine which he calls us roy come down

off the flagpole wavin while we dying. Tatatataaaa aaa (his

crooked horn national association of gungadins We will not be

interested in anything but cleanclothes and shined shoes. Better

(can you digit?) than Sheims ever were. YEH AND THEY MIGHT EVEN

HAVE LIGHTS ON THE MOTHERFUCKERS!

But it is only a value system (scripture/doctrine) that will save us. Its why the Koran was so heavy, for them. And the bible, for some other them. We need our own heavy book. Maybe it'll be a heavy "television" series or metaphysical '45s. We must have our doctrine, our new black quran to save us to lift us. This is why god is important, to keep you god like and the tone is god the result is godlike. We say dont smoke dont drink no dope blank on white women the entire body of europa is diseased. And dying. To survive you must draw away from it to what you are naturally anyway.

You are not the iceman brother.

Dont let him involve you

in his horrible ignominious dying.

Ideology and style are the same thing. You think Marx ever dressed like this dude in the black. Its about that. How to explain Trane to Trotsky. The feelin intended. Sun Ra is to teach Freud not the reverse. Freud is a child. We know old niggers hummin in the hall way, what can Shakespeare do with that, except Raise! Dig it.

So we are parts of a body. And this is what you see. The energy revealed. Its slow parts for you baby. And what is the changing same for us, the reality beneath illusion that binds us, as the body is bound by its motion its intent. From the kids the simbas to the old folks, sweet sisters in between, what will hold us in motion, with the content of the black chemist the black magician, the changers of what is to what must be, what but our selves. We are Africans brother. All of us. all over this planet, as we move to the next. Like Garvey and Malcolm have said, and Maulana Karenga has repeated, Africans, whatever that means. By Race and by Culture, by color and hopefully by consciousness, we can move with the deep old feeling of our ancient communion with unmanifest being, which is the final reality. And that was, and is blackness, god.

Look into my eyes. (These flicks.) Look into your own eyes. Hear the breath of divine music. Hear the pulse of the growth to control of all environment. We believe finally in ourselves as magic bearers and changers of reality to reality. All Praises To the Black Man.

If I have said anything of value, all praises due to you, Black People.

There is no you there is no *me*.

The different categories subside into the total which is all our strength, and all our weakness.

Memory is longer than the moment. In some states memory has bones and feet. Memory is actual pain actual pleasure. Check it out.

There are states of memory that receive the electhereal substances of postbody existence. They are characterized like M O cards in the police station by the dye of activity, the essence of whatever is existence. Prepare for longer states of existence than the one you going thru. This is what people been trying to tell you. Punishment, Blood? What you talking about? When its gonna come? It came. You are your own punishment. You and the devil. And he but a figment of your imagination. If you didn't want him here you would arrange for him to disappear. Check it out!

And all of us are one body, man. Dig it? One body. As each is a

small, as each of our organs is a small, and we, the large, so

the nation, is the large in relationship to us. And then the, like

they say, United Nations, then United Planets. Check it out. What

energy institutionalized will control the United Planets? Think

on it. We know these cities are ugly. We know they are examples

of white art. white feeling (?). So are the laws, the rule(s), the ethos,

the totality of that registration is white art, white artifact,

from white feeling. The Empire State Building is a white,

man.

(So what if you helped
build it. That ought to tell you
something. You damn sho dont
own nothin. Thass just your
electricity in their light bulbs
man. You must have the
institutions *the form,
and the reform*...which is
the refining to immortality.

Say all that to say We are the beautiful the hip the wise. For

real. But what does it all mean without the power, and nothing

near that comes to us, without the path, the backbone, i.e., the

value system. Faith, the fuel. Faith in Blackness

I love you black people

because I love my

self,

And you are that self, thrown big

against the heavens.

Cool brother must learn that the raw is the cool. And both benefit by unity as consciousness. So Jawbones and Charlie The Bass and Dewey and The Magi (plus they better all talk to Otis Granddad, he got the real word ... maybe even hip you to when Amen was the n of somebody ... like the bloods say A-a-Men ... A-a-Men ... A-a-Me A-Men, A-Men, thinking bout home. Ra could tell you about it too.)

But the announced thinkers
must force it. Must see to it.
Must collect their own consciousness
and project that as the spirit desired
in our swiftly animating nation.

Angry brother is angry at himself 1st. Or, ought to be. The

nigger he is, who is all. Each must have that consciousness.

The Devil is frightened by the blood w/his finger pointed only

because it makes the devil conscious of his own self. What we

say the mirror says much more precisely. And that little vestige

of larger self in the devil, tries to speak. Beast language, in

the darkness. And all the different versions of us here. Dig them,

and benefit. Pick up on another aspect of yr grace and wit and

delicate incisive motional hipness, Black People.

Dude with the pointing finger. Fuck you Dynamite Jim, or whatever

your name is! He cd be saying, arguing Fanon or w/DebilMoon about how

we gonna finally take over our own space in these same shitty

towns transforming them with our vision and style to be extensions

of swiftshake and stomp sound. The buildings will be attitudes,

vibrating like James Brown the ecstasy of the ultimate.

Dude with the little round glasses. You nationalists, If you
gonna be that, be it true. Let your dreams be plans for righteous
expansion of the people, and sure enough that will happen. Plan
and organize. Study, as Maulana says, Study. Think, Black. Dig
under the cripple surfaces of "things." The buildings crumble,
it is the spirit that motivates.

Not just idle screams (to work off the sensual connection with this rotten chapter of world).

But programs. Systems. Things that move and will grow. Living strategems to free and build. Political Projects. Communications Projects. Educational Projects. And on. Go head. Do it, if you gonna talk it. You better do it.

George too, know somethin's up. Us. Off the floor, please, not off the wall. The experience has been digested, and each of its particles assimilated by us. (Look into our eyes. Look into yr own eyes. Visualize yr own face, when you close yr eyes. Can you do that? Can you see your own image?)

The old man looks one way   the young blood looks another

Tho sometime it do get cold.
But when granddad cut out. I'm on the scene. And as far as that's
concerned the Simba's train everynight, to take up the slack. And
we got 20 month old Simbas and some still in the belly, some still
in the sparkle of big brown eyes. But the cycle is complete.
Goin and coming. Up and down sideways and backwards.
Its together. (Dude had on earmuffs.)

The past and the future. The circle complete. We gotcha goin both ways baby,

and aint gonna give up on nothin'. Its perfect. Think about it.

Black will be hip, and the heat generated

will cause the iceman to move "black"

pawns on the scene, to show off his own

"humanity". But it is an ascending scale

(See A Black Value System: "Spiritual Interpretations

of Maulana Karenga's Nguzo Saba") that cannot

be reached by fake. The pawns will be only that.

Tho we pray all our brothers become

conscious. Some will cry Black and still

have uncooked pork between they teeth

materially at night

and dreamily at day.

So the blood with the Agbada (robe) and the sisters with the

natural must also represent the consciousness

that change symbolizes. Dewey should know what I'm talking about.

(That other dude ought to stop smoking!) Life sitting there

looking for something to happen. Jawbones standing there with

the Simba over his shoulder, looking for something to happen.

Herman standing there, with a ring on, wow, knowing something
gotta happen. (He done blew the jail, smiling like he waitin
for a bus, when really is us he waiting for, and his self.

It's just a matter of time, the heat's on.

When the old sisters get to standing
there waitin for us. Been waitin for so long, like that endless patience (Man,
you better play both them numbers) all our souls can be seen.

We are the one vehicle of true faith.
The order of service. Is the whole black family. Now the old folks
waiting. This last old sister, if she was the judge, that look up
in your face, for real, like we say, everythings for real. So is
the cycle, and the illusion, and the reality. Everything. And yo
self, brother, you self, I know thats for real.

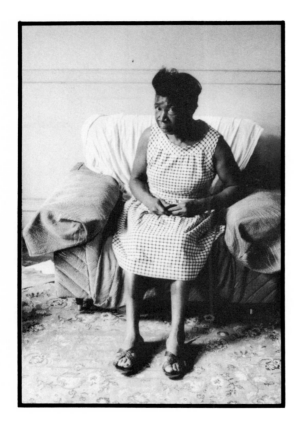

The old sister sits in her
endless patience, so that aspect of ourselves is valuable, for the
endurance, the unkillable, undiscourageable endurance

Like the
rage of the young brother, the swiftness the coolness of the Magi,
the realness of Jawbones, the beauty pure beauty of the sisters,
all of it, and Abernathy and me, and like this all is meant to
say. All praises due to you black people. You will endure and
survive and be the majestic rulers of all your space, again, if
you want to.

Now, sit (mama) and meditate . . . try to see your own face, when you close your eyes. Now call that name, of the figure you see, call that name the real sound your substance is. Call it deep inside yourself. The beginning. We all need to do the same. Then get your hat. i.e., get up and go

Allahu Akbar

Sifa ote Mtu Weusi

Adzhu billahi Mini Shatani

r Rajim

Imamu Amiri Baraka

IMAGES

(Order of Appearance)

Flight (The Glory of Hip)

Order of Service

The Screen

Paul

Black Power Youth (Kevin)

Friendly Scorpio Sister (Connie)

Uncrowned Queen

Love

More Than All

Manchild 1965 AM

Gaming

Halo Sky/Leather & Ring

Living Proof

Row of FOI

Toothpick In dus try Smiles

cats who are PEACOCKS strut

Trio of Flowers on 4 TRAY

Tooty Booty

Man

Original Hipster with Herbert in Background

COOL BREEZE (Bop do be do be dillia do be da da do be dopp woo daaaaa)

Saints Warriors & Heroes

Across the Street from Spirit House in LeRoi J's New Ark New J

Draped

Mothers Day

Jawbones & Paul

Redefinition

The Drummer

Lake Park Partners on Cottage Grove

At the End of Stirling Street

The Double Cover

Abshalom

Brother Carver

And We Own the Night (Subtle Smith Smile of Style)

Dewey

Charlie the Bass

Cousin Maurice

Herman

George

Old Man & Simba hence ETERNAL LOVE

I'm Coming Home

Independent Pride

Queen on her Throne